EXPLORING WORLD CULTURES

Singapore

Alicia Z. Klepeis

Cavendish Square

New York

Published in 2019 by Cavendish Square Publishing, LLC
243 5th Avenue, Suite 136, New York, NY 10016

Library of Congress Cataloging-in-Publication Data

Names: Klepeis, Alicia, 1971- author.
Title: Singapore / Alicia Z. Klepeis.
Description: First edition. | New York : Cavendish Square, 2019. |
Series: Exploring world cultures | Includes bibliographical references and index. | Audience: Grades 2-5.
Identifiers: LCCN 2018024821 (print) | LCCN 2018025142 (ebook) |
ISBN 9781502643575 (ebook) | ISBN 9781502643568 (library bound) |
ISBN 9781502643544 (pbk.) | ISBN 9781502643551(6 pack)
Subjects: LCSH: Singapore--Juvenile literature.
Classification: LCC DS609 (ebook) | LCC DS609 .K54 2019 (print) | DDC 959.57--dc23
LC record available at https://lccn.loc.gov/2018024821

Editorial Director: David McNamara
Editor: Lauren Miller
Copy Editor: Nathan Heidelberger
Associate Art Director: Alan Sliwinski
Designer: Christina Shults
Production Coordinator: Karol Szymczuk
Photo Research: J8 Media

Printed in the United States of America

Contents

Introduction

Singapore is the smallest country in Southeast Asia. People have lived in Singapore for hundreds of years. Different people have ruled it. Today, Singapore is independent. Singapore is also unique. It is both a country and a city. That makes it a **city-state**.

People who live in Singapore are called Singaporeans. They have many different jobs. Lots of Singaporeans work in stores, banks, hotels, or schools. They enjoy playing sports. Soccer and badminton are popular. Swimming and other water sports are common too. Singaporeans enjoy music and dancing. They have many special traditions and celebrations. The country is famous for its food.

Singapore has beautiful places to visit. There are wetlands, beaches, and many parks. The city of Singapore is nicknamed the Garden City. Tourists come to see the nation's gardens and **nature reserves**. Tropical flowers bloom here all year.

Singapore is an amazing country to explore.

The cityscape of Singapore city has many tall skyscrapers and bright lights.

Singapore is an **archipelago**, or group of islands. It is located south of Malaysia and Thailand. The Johor Strait and the Singapore Strait surround it.

This map shows the major islands of Singapore.

Singapore covers 278 square miles (719 square kilometers). Singapore does not have any other countries connected to it. Malaysia and Indonesia are close neighbors though.

Singapore has a hot and humid climate all year. On average, it rains about 167 days each year.

Much of Singapore is flat. The nation's highest point is a hill called Bukit Timah, at 545 feet (166 meters). Some of Singapore's skyscrapers are taller than that!

A woman looks at dugongs at an aquarium.

Two important rivers in Singapore are the Kallang River and the Singapore River. In the 1800s, most of the country was covered in rain forests. Today, only about 3 percent of the land has forests.

Singapore's Wildlife

Singapore is home to many plants and animals. **Dugongs** and banded leaf monkeys live here. Thousands of plant species grow in Singapore too.

Sir Thomas Stamford Raffles (1781-1826)

People have lived in Singapore for hundreds of years. In the 1300s, people living there traded with other countries. They traded with Thailand, India, and China.

In 1819, a man named Sir Thomas Stamford Raffles arrived in Singapore and made it a British colony. He built a trading port for ships and traders from Asia, Africa, and Arabia. They traded with Singaporeans.

FACT!

There are only three recognized city-states today: Singapore, Monaco, and the Vatican City.

Lee Kuan Yew

Lee Kuan Yew was Singapore's first prime minister. He led the country for more than thirty years.

By the early 1900s, Singapore was a modern city. During World War II, Japan took control. It was a tough time for Singaporeans. After the war, Singapore became a British colony again. Then Singapore was part of Malaysia. Finally, Singapore became its own country in 1965.

Lee Kuan Yew (*center*) was Singapore's first prime minister.

Today, Singapore is a successful country. Many of its people have good and happy lives.

9

VOTE ✓

Singapore's government is unique. The country is not divided into sections, or states. Singapore is a city-state. That means it is a country and a city.

Singapore's Parliament House.

Singapore's government has three parts: legislative, judicial, and executive. The legislative part is called Parliament. Parliament has 101 members. They work in Parliament House. There, they write new laws and keep track of the government's money.

FACT!

All Singaporean citizens over twenty-one years old must vote in elections.

Halimah Yacob

Singapore's first female president was Halimah Yacob. She became president in September 2017.

President Halimah Yacob is a Malay Muslim.

The judicial part is made up of courts. They follow the country's constitution. The constitution describes all the basic laws of Singapore. It was adopted in 1965.

The prime minister, president, and **cabinet** ministers make up the executive part. The prime minister runs the government. The president is the leader of the country. He or she is sometimes called the head of state.

Singapore has one of the largest economies in Southeast Asia. It trades with countries like China, Malaysia, Indonesia, and the United States.

An employee works in a Singaporean factory that makes cell phones.

Most Singaporeans have service jobs. Some work in museums, shops, and banks. Others have jobs in restaurants, hotels, and schools. Tourism is important to this small nation. People come from all over the world to see

FACT!

Over seventeen million tourists visited Singapore from other countries in 2017.

Money in Singapore

Singaporeans pay with items using the Singapore dollar. The money is colorful. Images of people and places from Singapore's history are on the dollar.

A close-up of Singapore's colorful money.

the Gardens by the Bay and visit the Singapore Zoo.

Factories in Singapore make items like batteries, shoes, and parts for computers and smartphones.

Unlike most countries, farming is not common in Singapore. As of 2017, less than 1 percent of land was used for farming. The farmers in Singapore grow vegetables and raise chickens and fish.

The Environment

Singapore's people, animals, and plants need clean water and air to live. Some places in Singapore don't have these things.

Haze caused by burning forests in Indonesia during September 2015.

Air pollution is a serious problem. Some of this pollution comes from cars and factories in Singapore. Other pollution comes from other countries. The nearby country of Indonesia burns

FACT!

Because Singapore is very urban, animals like the Sunda pangolin are becoming more rare. Today, many animals are protected by the government.

Singapore and Energy

Singapore gets more than 98 percent of its electricity from burning gas and coal. In the future, the country hopes to use more solar power. Solar and wind are much better for the planet.

forests. These fires can cover Singapore in a layer of smoke. They make the air in Singapore difficult to breathe.

A mother and baby Sunda pangolin on display at Singapore's Night Safari.

Singapore also does not have a lot of freshwater. A lot of Singapore's freshwater comes from Malaysia. Singapore is trying to make its water cleaner and safer to use.

Over 5.6 million people live in Singapore. Family is very important there. Grandparents or other close relatives often live with families in the same apartment

Kids attend a class at the Singapore Olympic Academy.

or apartment building. Marriage is also important to Singaporean society. It is encouraged from a young age.

Singapore is home to different **ethnic groups**. Chinese people make up about 74 percent of Singaporeans. Most of these people had family members who moved to Singapore. They wanted a new life. Malaysians make up about 13 percent of Singaporeans. Many people think the Malay were the first people to live in Singapore. Around 9 percent of people in Singapore are Indian.

Singapore's ethnic groups have their own traditions, celebrations, and shopping areas. For example, Little India is filled with shops that sell Indian clothes, flowers, and snacks.

The Peranakan People

The Peranakan people have Chinese and Malay/Indonesian ancestors. Peranakans are known for their food. They also have their own style of dress and jewelry.

17

Almost all of Singapore's people live in tall apartment buildings in the city. The government built many of these. Very few people live in their own houses.

Most Singaporeans live in large apartment buildings.

Children in Singapore attend primary school for six years. After, they can choose between regular school and specialized school. There are specialized schools for the arts, sports, math, and science.

Singapore has lots of green space. In fact, parks and gardens make up 47 percent of the city.

People in the city can walk to work, take a bus or train, or ride a bike. Some Singaporeans drive cars to work. However, most people use public transit because it is cheaper.

A public transport bus pulls into a station in Singapore.

Families that live in the city usually have cell phones and televisions. Most people use the internet. Singapore is a very high-tech nation!

Women in the Workforce

Around 60 percent of Singaporean women have jobs. Some companies let women work from home. That helps them balance work and family life.

Religion

Religion is an important part of some Singaporeans' lives. While there is not an official religion, about one-third of the people here are Buddhist. They pray in temples or at shrines in their homes. Singaporean

At this Chinese shrine, pineapples are left as an offering.

Buddhists celebrate Vesak Day in the spring. This day celebrates Buddha. It is a time of reflection, peace, and joy.

FACT!

Over 16 percent of people in Singapore are not religious.

Sultan Mosque

Singapore's Sultan Mosque was first built in 1824. The current building was finished in 1932. Its prayer hall can hold up to five thousand people.

Sultan Mosque is located on Arab Street in Singapore.

Just over 14 percent of Singaporeans are Muslim. They worship in mosques.

Singapore has other religious groups too. There are large Christian and Hindu populations. Over 11 percent of Singaporeans are Taoist. Taoism is an ancient religion from China. It includes a number of gods and goddesses. There are also some people who do not believe in a religion.

Language

Singapore has four official languages. They are Malay, Mandarin, English, and Tamil. Malay is often considered the national language of Singapore. This is because Singapore and Malaysia have a

Road signs in Singapore are usually written in two or more languages.

common history. Both countries were once ruled by the same people.

FACT!

Chinese Singaporeans have their family name (what we call a last name) first, followed by their given (or first) name.

Singlish

Many people in Singapore use an informal language called Singlish. It combines English with words from Chinese, Malay, and Tamil.

Chinese Singaporeans often speak Mandarin or other **dialects** like Hokkien and Cantonese. Tamil is spoken by Indian Singaporeans.

English is the language that connects all Singaporeans. The government uses English. Businesses also use English. Children are taught English in schools.

Most Singaporeans read and write in at least two languages. For many, English is their second language. Newspapers in Singapore are written in all four official languages.

Art is important to people in Singapore. In the city, there are lots of outdoor sculptures. Tourists often visit the famous Orchard Art Trail. It has many examples of modern art.

The Supertree Garden is a popular tourist attraction at Gardens by the Bay.

Dance is also popular. Akar Subur is an event where Malay dances are performed. They combine both traditional and modern dance moves.

Singaporean artists make many types of music. The Singapore Symphony Orchestra plays classical music. There are also modern pop artists from Singapore like Dick Lee and Kelly Poon.

In 2013, *Ilo Ilo* was the first Singaporean feature film to win the Camera d'Or award at the Cannes Film Festival. This award is given to the best film by a new director.

Singapore has festivals all year round. One major holiday is National Day on August 9. This day celebrates Singapore's independence from Malaysia.

National Gallery Singapore

Visit the National Gallery Singapore and you will see the world's biggest collection of modern Southeast Asian art.

There are lots of ways to have fun in Singapore. People like to run and swim. Group sports like soccer, badminton, and basketball are popular. Many Singaporeans belong to local sports

A family kayaks along Singapore's coast.

groups. They are called leagues. There are also national teams for basketball, soccer, and cricket.

FACT!

Singapore is known for its many shopping malls. Orchard Road alone has over thirty malls in just 1.4 miles (2.2 kilometers).

Olympic Gold

Singaporean swimmer Joseph Schooling won a gold medal at the 2016 Olympics. He won the men's 100-meter butterfly race.

Joseph Schooling won an Olympic gold medal in Brazil in 2016.

Sailing, waterskiing, and kayaking are popular. People can try wakeboarding at Singapore Wake Park or paddleboarding along the coast.

Many Singaporeans enjoy playing games. Kuti Kuti is a traditional kids' game. Two players try to flip colorful plastic pieces on top of their opponent's pieces. If one person's piece lands on top of the other person's piece, they win both pieces.

27

Chicken rice is often served with cucumber or sliced tomatoes.

Around the globe, Singapore is famous for its food.

The Chinese, Malay, and Indian Singaporeans each have their own recipes. For example, a popular Chinese dish is called chicken rice. The rice is cooked in chicken broth. It is served with chicken and a sauce made of ginger, soy sauce,

FACT!

Hawker centers are open-air food courts that are very popular in Singapore.

An Unusual Dessert

Chendol is a popular dessert in Singapore. It's made with coconut milk, shaved ice, red beans, palm sugar, and tiny bits of **pandan-**flavored jelly.

and chilies. Some say that this is the national dish. Others say it's fish head curry or chili crab.

Thanks to the tropical weather, people in Singapore enjoy many kinds of fruit. Papaya and mangoes grow there. So do the spiky, smelly fruits called durians.

Glossary

archipelago   A group of islands.

cabinet   A group of advisors who help the leader of a government.

city-state   A self-governing country made up of a city and its surrounding territory.

dialects   Forms of a language used by people in a specific social group or region.

dugongs   Mammals that are related to manatees. They eat plants and live in water, and live for up to seventy years.

ethnic groups   Groups of people who share a common culture or ancestry.

nature reserves Protected land for plants and animals.

pandan   The fruit of a tropical shrub or tree (sometimes called screw pine).

Find Out More

Books

Lowbeer, Michelle. *ABC Explore Singapore*. Singapore: Marshall Cavendish International, 2018.

Owings, Lisa. *Singapore*. Minneapolis, MN: Bellwether Media, 2014.

Website

Singapore Travel Guide

https://www.nationalgeographic.com/travel/destinations/asia/singapore

Video

Singapore: City Video Guide

https://www.youtube.com/watch?v=ocg80OZvkMw

Index

About the Author

Alicia Z. Klepeis began her career at the National Geographic Society. She is the author of many kids' books, including *Building Mount Rushmore*, *Snakes Are Awesome*, and *A Time for Change*. She visited Singapore when she was in college and cannot wait to return.